Praise for *From Pa*

"God truly does turn our pa[...] [...]nto [...]urpose if we let Him! This book is a demonstration of Jessika's commitment to the process of allowing the pain from her past and her story of overcoming it to inspire and encourage others!"

—**Harmony Grillo**, Founder,
Treasures Ministry

"If you are looking for a thorough and practical way to reset after a life altering event, you will not be disappointed! You will be encouraged every step of the way. Jessika shares vulnerably, creating space for the reader to connect to the deepest parts of themselves. A must read for anyone desiring to discover their purpose in life."

—**Monique Calderón-Remenda**,
Tedx Talker and Advocate with Zoe International

"*From Pain to Purpose* is heartfelt and strategy packed! Jessika provides a roadmap with everyday practices to travel this journey *From Pain to Purpose* and to ultimately improve your life! Throughout this book you not only get to read about Jessika's personal experiences that lead her to finding her own true purpose but you also get to read and be reminded of God's words through scripture and Hebrew biblical context. I recommend this book for anybody looking to find true meaning in their own lives and feeling alone in their pain or struggles."

—**Nola Kesia Brantley-Harris**, CEO,
Nola Brantley Speaks

FROM PAIN
TO PURPOSE

FROM PAIN TO PURPOSE

How to Return to Purpose After Experiencing Trauma or Loss

Jessika Fuhrmaneck

NASHVILLE

NEW YORK • LONDON • MELBOURNE • VANCOUVER

From Pain to Purpose

How to Return to Purpose After Experiencing Trauma or Loss

Published in New York, New York, by Morgan James Publishing. Morgan James is a trademark of Morgan James, LLC. www.MorganJamesPublishing.com

ISBN 9781642799613 paperback
ISBN 9781642799620 eBook
Library of Congress Control Number: 2019956399

Cover Design by:
Jonathan Lewis
jonathan@jonlincreative.com

Interior Design by:
Melissa Farr
melissa@backporchcreative.com

Morgan James is a proud partner of Habitat for Humanity Peninsula and Greater Williamsburg. Partners in building since 2006.

Get involved today! Visit
MorganJamesPublishing.com/giving-back

This book is dedicated to all the survivors, those who overcame loss, trauma, death of loved ones, and physical pain, the women who have experienced abuse and exploitation and found their way back to their purpose, the men who have seen violence and lived to love life in spite of the darkness.

Every page of this book is written for you. Every word carefully chosen so that you might know that you were never alone. That God and others understand you, remember you, and that I believe you can and will find your way back to your calling. My dream for all of you is that you will not just survive but thrive.

The proceeds of this book are specially dedicated to www.FromPainToPurpose.org for the benefit of survivors of sexual exploitation and human trafficking.

Contents

Acknowledgments

Thank you Roe and Jim Dodgen for being with me every step of the way on this healing journey. With out your input and advice I would probably still be dating my ex and have little understanding of my true value and honor as a woman.

Harmony and Chris you have both been a special part of my life. To see two of my friends fall in love with each other was one of the most inspiring things I have ever witnessed in my life! I thank you both for standing by me during those heart-breaking moments when my life crashed down around me. Your words of wisdom and hope still ring in my ears today. Thank you for loving me through the process. You are both so very precious to me.

Monique Calderón! Oh my word, where would I be with out you! You entered my life when I had recently lost my hopes and dreams, but you saw in me a fierceness I couldn't even see in myself. You have continually prayed for me and spoken words of encouragement to me when I was in my darkest moments. You have never lost hope for my life. You are a true friend, and because of your immense faith I am able to be a force to help other women who have also been exploited and forgotten. Thank you for loving me so fiercely and faithfully!

Mom and Sis – oh how your hearts must have broken when you witnessed my life fall to pieces around me. Many years ago my then pastor Robert Flores said to me "Friends take sides." I remembered those words as I watched people hold on tight to their love for me, as others were sifted out of my life. You have both stood firm in your commitment to love and protect and help me in any way you can. You are amazing women and I am grateful to call you family. I love you both so much.

Thanks to my publishing team David Hancock, Jim Howard, Bethany Marshall, Nickcole Watkins, Amber Parrott, Taylor Chaffer, Bonnie Rauch, and Karen Anderson! I couldn't have done it without your encouragement and assistance! You brought my dream to a tangible reality and your guidance and patience meant so much to me!

Introduction

Years ago on one lovely January afternoon in Southern California the road of my life suddenly reached a brick wall. I was sitting in a counseling session with my boyfriend and our pastor. We met two months after I began attending a local church in Los Angeles, California. I had recently gone through a divorce and he swooped right in and became a self-appointed savior. Every thing I needed he provided. A place to do my laundry, a truck to drive, a ride to work, and job opportunities. He quickly had his hand in everything I was doing.

The odd thing is I never asked him for help with any of those things. I didn't want to be rescued; I wanted a partner in life. Some one I could confide in and also have fun with. I wanted a man I could walk out my God given purpose with in a way that would empower both of us. Because of promises he made to me, I thought that this man would become that partner.

My expectation was that we would leave this counseling session and walk back out in to the sunny seventy-degree California weather with a clear path toward marriage. I was speechless when the pastor suggested we take a six-month break. I literally could not speak for hours.

In the year after that 'brick wall' moment God began to prepare me for my life's purpose. I slowly walked in to my true identity and my true destiny. Many times in my life my purpose and destiny had been confused and corrupted by others. But on this day I was set free.

Where is *your* life headed? Have you experienced an ending, or loss, and can't see the road anymore? Join us on this journey to understand who you were made to be, and set your purpose to align with the dream for your life.

Let Go Of Your Dreams

When I went through my 'Esther year', as I so fondly like to call it, I didn't even know what was happening to me. I started the year with no goals, nothing I wanted to manifest. I was stressed out and rejected. For the first time in many years I did not sit down on the first of January and write out my goals. I think I felt as though I had done that so diligently the last few years just to have the things I wanted most continue to evade me.

Throughout the year, every once in a while I would think, "I better set a goal for this year." But, I never did. And I'm glad I didn't because essentially what happened was I allowed myself to be guided in a direction I couldn't have found on my own. Out of this year of God preparing me, came *From Pain to Purpose*.

Now, I'm not suggesting that you begin each year with no goals or plans. However, let's always remember to leave wiggle room for God to do a miracle.

I used to work with an outreach leader named Ashley. When we were about to enter in to a big day that we had planned she would often pray "Lord, wreck this day if you so will it." I loved that prayer. In life we can prepare, but we don't always see the bigger picture. We don't know what unscheduled moments will happen throughout our day. If we can learn to allow our story to unfold we will find ourselves uniquely placed in positions where we can use our gifts and talents to create real change in the world around us.

I'm excited to share this book with you. This book is my miracle—my big change. I'm excited for what's going to come in the next year as you journey through life, connected to the spirit of your creator, to be prepared for what you were uniquely designed to do, and also what you uniquely have to offer the world around you. *Let's begin!*

This book was inspired by the story of Queen Esther, which can be found in the Hebrew Tanakh. Esther was orphaned, but she was not left abandoned. A relative adopted her as his daughter when her parents died. This might have been her brick wall moment. No child plans to lose both of their parents, just as I expected my boyfriend to always be there, as he had promised. We have moments in life when what we thought was secure and foundational turns out to be sand beneath our feet, which is so easily washed away in the tide. After our dreams are pulled away from us, ripped out of our hands by forces that feel stronger than us, we must eventually find our way to solid ground. The danger in this moment is staring endlessly at the sea looking for a dream that has long since washed away.

Esther, the orphan, was eventually made queen. But before she was chosen for that role she spent a year being guided and prepared. This is your year. You too will set aside this time to being prepared and aligned with the purpose and destiny meant for your life here on this beautiful blue planet. Just as Esther had Mordecai and Hegai to help her become the queen the people needed, you too will have helpers along the way to guide you and show you the steps needed to walk in your purpose. I don't know what your calling in life is, but I can promise you that part of your purpose will be helping others in a way that you are uniquely designed to.

If you're feeling lost, if you're feeling like nothing you have tried has worked, you have opened the right book. I felt the same way when I started opening my heart to God's ideas for my life. I truly had no faith that anything I tried would work, because I had put every thing I had in to preparing for a life with my future husband and I had nothing to show for it.

If you have been doing well, but just want to take it to the next level, and discern your purpose even more clearly, you too are in the right place. Welcome, I'm glad you're here, and I can't wait to see how your story unfolds.

What was most interesting to me about Esther's story was that she prepared diligently never knowing that she would actually be chosen as queen. What she did know was that she was chosen for a specific purpose. Mordacai adopted her and rescued her from life as an orphan. He treated her as his own special and valuable daughter. What I find to be probably the most important part of being able to get from where you are now to where you want to be is letting spirit guide you. Esther allowed Mordacai to advise her. She trusted his words. She allowed safe and trustworthy people in her life to guide her and take care of her, and prepare her.

Are you ready to let God show you your next step? In my experience it's quite common that desires will arise within your heart that feel impossible. You will likely be inspired to take actions that might not make sense in your own understanding. It's important to remember that the spirit of our creator lives within you. It may be hard to understand or comprehend, but we *are* empowered to do all that we feel destined to do.

"As the heavens are higher than the earth, so are my ways higher than your ways and my thoughts than your thoughts."
Isaiah 55:9

The first thing I'm going to ask you to do is to *give up*. Sounds like bad advice, I know. It certainly doesn't sound like something a successful person would do; but giving up was the only way for me to walk in to my destiny and calling. I was asked at the very beginning of my year to give up that which was most important to me; that which was nearest to my heart, my biggest desire. Only, in this way was I able to walk in to the life and power that I was always meant to have.

If you follow the recommendations in this book diligently, and ask the spirit to intervene in your life throughout this year, I believe you will be able to reset the desire of your heart to a place where being in connection with God is your biggest and greatest pursuit. And once you have that, you will never feel empty again, because no one can ever take that connection away from us. We will never lose God. God will never break our heart. Our creator is a constant and rock solid foundation. Without this foundation, it will be difficult to build a legacy, or a destiny and become a queen or king.

So, let's take a deep dive and look at what you might need to let go of. Let me first state that attending church or being saved does not mean you have made connecting to your creator the desire of your heart. I was saved for years before my Esther year. I followed church teaching. I followed church law (mostly, no human is perfect). But, if the spirit nudged me, or I felt convicted about something, I was more than capable of ignoring that intuition when it didn't suit me. I could easily come up with reasons why it made no sense to do what I sensed I was supposed to do.

The biggest desire of my heart was not to connect and then co-create with God. For me the biggest desires of my heart were to have a husband and children, and on a more subconscious level to be accepted by my community. I was comparing, comparing, comparing, and when that didn't work, I rejected myself on many levels or found people to place in my life who would do it for me. By the time I started my year of preparations to be a queen I could barely hear God's voice anymore. All I could hear was my will to make happen what I wanted to happen. But, I never could make it happen.

There are a few things we are going to work on in this session. Let's list them!

1. Give up. Dig deep and ask yourself what is the biggest desire of your heart. What is the thing that is your treasure? Is it your husband, or wish to have a husband? Is it your children, or your future children? Is it your career, or your wish to be acknowledged for your successes?

   It might be helpful to sit quietly in a dimly lit room, and ask spirit to reveal to you the one thing, or even two things that are the true desires of your heart.

Now, once you've got them, imagine holding it so tightly in your hand. See your dream sitting in the palm of your hand and squeeze your fist tightly around it. Next I want you to imagine opening your hand and there is nothing there. It's gone! Your biggest dream, your biggest desire is gone. What do you feel? Do you feel panic? Do you feel like you're not sure who you are or what to do now without your dream? That's ok. Allow yourself to feel this.

If you don't feel much, then it might not have been your biggest dream. It should frighten you to give this dream up. It might even make you feel like you don't know who you are without it. That's good. This is where the work begins.

Now, you might be thinking "But doesn't God want us to have the desires of our heart?" I believe that is true. I believe our dreams are put in our heart for good reason. But when someone gives you a gift, their hope is that you will still value them more than the gift you were given. If I bought you a new shiny car, and you completely ignored me after that, I would most likely regret having given you that gift.

Also, how would it have turned out if they made Esther queen on the first day she arrived at the palace? She spent an entire year receiving treatments and healthy food to strengthen her. Both her adopted father Mordecai, and her caretaker Hegai gave her advice on how to behave and what to do. If they had made her queen on day one she most likely would have been overwhelmed and lacked the knowledge needed to make the choices a queen must ultimately make. When we receive things we are not ready for, it is not a blessing at all. It takes time, care, and training to walk in to our life's purpose. Let's take that time to become all that we were born to be.

Sometimes in order for God to bless us and bring us to our purpose we need to get out of the way. Esther was open to Mordecai's advice, Hagai's recommendations, and certainly other attendants who were helping with this process along the way. What if she had said, "No, I got this, I know what to do, I don't need your help." She wouldn't have learned much that way.

So give up your dreams. Just for now. And do it sincerely. I promise you if you are still holding on to it you will find yourself struggling through this year. Even if it takes weeks, or months, keep giving it up until it no longer has power over you. I personally struggled with letting go of my dream for my life. I had to frequently pray for help. So, set that intention, and just keep returning to it if you feel like you're holding on again at any point. Release, release, release, open up your fists and release!

2. Confess. Un-confessed deeds will hinder your prayers. Un-confessed wrongs keep you from closeness with your creator. If you have been hiding a secret, find a counselor, a pastor, a mentor, or a sponsor to confess it to. In Celebrate Recovery they have a saying. "We are as sick as our secrets." If you go in to this year harboring a secret, big or small, then you are going to struggle to truly deeply experience change and freedom. Take some time. Sit down, and figure out what your secrets are. Be sure that you are confessing it to a safe person. Do not tell someone who is going to share it with others or be judgmental. This really should be some one in a position to help or counsel you if need be.

In my case, I confessed a secret that had ramifications for both myself and another person. By the time I confessed I was truly sick of holding on to my secret. I had also given myself months to prepare for the consequences of confessing. And there were consequences. If this secret is something that will change your life make sure you have people in place that will help you navigate the process. By the time I confessed I had a team of people to support me. Take some time to build that team, but set a goal to have made the confession no later than six weeks in to this year.

3. If you do not already belong to a recovery-based program, do some research and see what groups you feel you might benefit from. There are lots of twelve-step programs, small groups, or even a grief recovery class. It may serve you to be involved in some kind of evaluative style of recovery for at least six months. If you are planning to make a commitment to take a break from dating or some other type of fast, I recommend you do it in the beginning of this journey rather than later in the process. We want to

get things up and out before we start building a new foundation.

4. Lastly, let's have some fun with fashion! This time of preparation is not designed to work only on your insides. It's for the outsides too! One thing I want you to never loose sight of during this process is having fun!

Ok, so have you surrendered your dreams? Have you created a plan to confess your secrets to a safe person? Have you chosen a recovery-based program you'd like to join? If the answer is yes, yes, and yes, you may now proceed with this final step for Session 1.

What we wear affects how we feel. I want you to take an hour and lay out your entire wardrobe. You are molding yourself in to a queen or king this year. Do you have a wardrobe that causes you to feel strong, important, healthy, valuable, and respectable? When I first did this I tried to imagine and consider how important and carefully chosen a queen's wardrobe is. I encourage you to have that same attitude with your own wardrobe.

I found the *Personal Seasonal Color Analysis* to be very useful in helping me decide what items should be a part of my wardrobe. Some of you may already be familiar with this concept. Is it a way to help us choose colors to wear in order to compliment our unique hair and skin tones. We are going to review four main categories, and you will find you can place your particular skin and hair coloring in to one of these categories.

There are lots of websites that I have used to help me determine my best color palette. Some have charts similar to the one below. If you enjoy wearing makeup, there are websites that will suggest which makeup colors to wear. Just search for 'personal seasonal color analysis' on Google, and you should be able to find all the information you need!

I made this helpful questionnaire to get you started, but I really encourage you to take the time to investigate further on your own.

- Do you look better in navy blue, charcoal grey, honey beige, or soft brown?
- Do you have natural blonde hair, brunette, or red hair?
- Do you have blue eyes, pale eyes, or dark eyes?
- Pale blue eyes with navy blue or charcoal = Summer Color Palette
- Deep blue eyes with navy blue or charcoal = Winter Color Palette

- Beige or brown with blonde and pale eyes = Spring Color Palette
- Beige or brown with dark eyes, brunette or red hair = Autumn Color Palette

Don't stop here! There are many outlets to help us determine our best style. I sometimes search for a description of what I want to convey and see what comes up. For example you might search 'classy and strong', or 'fun and hip'. See what ideas this spurs!

It doesn't have to be expensive. Determine what your wardrobe budget is, and stick to it. Over spending will only cause stress. There are lots of stores that have discounted prices. I also like to go to swap parties, or just post online that I'm looking for extra clothes, and sticking to a budget. You'd be surprised how much clothes your friends are looking to unload! But stick to your color palette. Don't take it just because it's free. If it doesn't actually look good on you leave it for someone else who would benefit from that particular outfit.

Take your time working through these four tasks. Sign up for a recovery program in your area. And have some fun with your wardrobe! I hope you have enjoyed your first session of going *From Pain to Purpose*!

Let's Eat Some Food!

Congratulations! You made it through Session 1, and I hope you had some fun along the way! Session 2 will begin a three-part process to address your body, mind, and spiritual state. We're going to take some time to create balance and improve healthy habits.

"Therefore everyone who hears these words of mine and puts them into practice is like a wise wo/man who built her/his house on the rock. The rain came down, the streams rose, and the winds blew and beat against that house; yet it did not fall, because it had its foundation on the rock."
Matthew 7:24-27

I spent many years in recovery, working through mental, emotional, and spiritual scars. I learned a great deal, and I definitely grew. However, I sometimes found that I repeated cycles, going back to the beginning over and over. It was when I was writing a session for a parenting program that I discovered Maslow's Hierarchy of Needs. This pyramid suggests that if certain things are established first, the foundation for the rest is much stronger. Take a look at the numbered list below, with self-actualization representing the highest level.

Self-
Actualization
Level 4, Achievements
Level 3, Love and Belonging
Level 2, Safety Needs (security, safety)
Level 1, Physiological Needs (food, water, warmth, rest)

I realized over time that I frequently skipped level 1 and 2 and started my days searching for 3 and above. But, I often felt overwhelmed, or embarrassed. If I actually established a relationship with a man or a new friend, I couldn't have them over because the house was a mess. I also suffered from low blood sugar or deficiencies from not taking time out to eat. So, if I tried to write or create I couldn't think clearly.

I eventually came to the conclusion that it's best to meet these five needs in the listed order to sustain growth in my life. It's easy to have spurts of energy or inspiration, but to maintain steady momentum in life we have to build on a foundation. We can't build the house from the roof down.

For me, patience was always a challenge. I did not finish well, and I found myself in my thirties with a lot of broken dreams. At any age, you can begin to create a firm foundation. It is not too soon, it is not too late. We can begin co-creating with God at any point in our lives. You have not missed anything.

You are going to learn how to take care of your body in a way you can understand and manage long term. We are going to build that physiological foundation over the next couple of sessions. This is the longest we will focus on one subject but the foundation of any pyramid takes more stones than the levels above it. So, take your time with these sessions, and invite God in to this part of the process. Say an intentional prayer to yourself, like the one below.

"Creator, God, Spirit, be with me as I build this very important foundation for my life. Help me to have patience and to hear your voice as I experience each day. Show me what areas to focus on, and help me to have fun while I do it! Bring me good friends, and sisters and brothers to walk along side me, and encourage me as I go!"

This month we are going to talk about food. Just as Esther took a year to prepare to be the queen, we too are going to take a closer look at the care of our bodies first and foremost.

I have learned a lot over the years about what to eat and what to avoid. Here is what I have found to be the most basic and healthy balanced diet. I preface this by saying that I am not a doctor. These are meant to be received as helpful suggestions and not an expert medical opinion. If you have a specific health issue please speak with your physician and adjust your meal plan accordingly.

1. **Eat six times a day at designated times.** I have found that if my meals are carefully planned, my body is able to burn the fuel at a steady pace with out building up unnecessary fat. I eat at 8am, 10am,

12pm, 2pm, 4pm, and 6pm. When I first started this habit I actually set 6 alerts in my phone that recurred every single day for three months. Let's do that together right now.

Pick up your phone. Add the word 'Eat' at each of those times. Set a reminder to repeat every day for at least the next thirty days.

In order for this to work you definitely have to pack your food. Some people find it helpful to cook and pack and freeze the week's food on Sunday night. Some cook and pack the evening before. Some have time to do it all every morning. Find a realistic strategy that will work for your schedule.

2. **Eat portions.** The 8am, 12pm, and 4pm meals are breakfast, lunch, and dinner. Each of these meals should have four ounces of protein, one cup of vegetables, half cup of grain or starch, and one tablespoon of oil.

Here's an example:

Breakfast: 2 eggs, 1 toast, butter, 1 cup of spinach.
Lunch: 1 cup of chopped vegetables, ½ cup of diced chicken, 1 tablespoon of dressing, ½ cup of rice.

Dinner: 1 cup steamed vegetables, ½ cup pasta, 4 ounces of meat, 1 tablespoon of olive oil.

An easy way to gauge these measurements is to have a half plate of vegetables, a quarter plate of meat, and a quarter plate of grains or potatoes.

3. **Eat certain foods at certain times.** Fruit should be eaten before noon because it has a lot of sugars and you want to burn through that over the course of the day. I have a half-cup of fruit at 10am.

   We need healthy fat in our diet. The best time to have that is as an afternoon pick-me-up. A handful of almonds are a great option.

   At 6pm I stick to lower calorie foods since I have little time left to burn this fuel. I might eat two cups of popcorn, or slices of cucumber with hummus.

4. **Be flexible!** We are living life with other people in it. Don't be the weird one who refuses to eat any thing served at events. When I am at a meeting, or dinner with friends I just remember what I would normally eat around that time and try to find that in the selection. If there are fruit and donuts offered, eat the fruit. If there are tacos and ribs being served,

eat a half-cup of ribs, and try to find a side dish like vegetables or rice.

It's not going to be perfect, but I don't have to eat a full plate of ribs and macaroni. There are always choices everywhere we go.

Also, it's nice to plan in fun items. For example, I like to have one dessert a week. If you are going to a holiday party, plan to eat your Mom's famous cherry pie that night. People love to be appreciated for their cooking. There is always a way to include tradition and still be healthy.

When it comes to big holidays I don't even sweat it. I will start with a balanced plate, but I will add a tablespoon of other sides that I want to at least taste on Thanksgiving. Instead of a second helping I bring a Tupperware and take home leftovers that I can eat the next day. That way I have something to look forward to.

You got this! Flexibility is key! Happy eating!!

Releasing Trauma Through Training

Let's talk about exercise. I have noticed that on Maslow's Pyramid, at no point is mood mentioned. I've lived through several different types of trauma and loss. Even after continuing mental and emotional care I sometimes have down days. Moving my body has been one of the most effective ways to balance my mood.

Training my body has been more of a spiritual and emotional goal for me than vanity ever could be. Being a queen or a king is not dependant on the shape of our bodies. Walking with confidence and authority is more about understanding our value.

I was exploited for twelve years in the commercial sex trade as a stripper. Prior to that, in my teen years, I was a swimwear model. Being presented as a physical object to be judged by others had a profound effect on how I relate to my body. I am very careful not to equate my value with how big my muscles are, or how slim my stomach is.

My goal is to be healthy and strong. I encourage you to remove words like 'skinny' or 'fat' from your vocabulary. I have had many friends refer to me as skinny as if it were a compliment. It never feels like a compliment to me when I am labeled as skinny. There is a proverb that says the power of life and death is in the tongue.

"From the fruit of her/his mouth a wo/man's stomach is filled;
with the harvest from her/his lips s/he is satisfied.
The tongue has the power of life and death,
and those who live it will eat its fruit."
Proverbs 18:20-21

Years ago I started correcting people when they spoke false declarations over my body. Now, if anyone refers to the size or shape of my body I respond by saying "I would prefer if you do not comment on my body." For me, this has been a crucial part of my healing process after being treated as an object or product for so many years.

As we begin to talk about healthy options for training our bodies, we want to make sure that we first understand the motive behind the workout. If your motive is to look good, to get the guy or girl, or to feel better about yourself, dig a little deeper for a healthier inspiration. These motivations likely won't endure over time.

Every morning I read affirmations to myself. One of them is "I am healthy and strong." This is a great primary motivation for my training. It focuses on self-love and self-care, which is something that will last through out my lifetime. Find a motivation that means something to you and write it down or record it in your phone so that you can look back on it as you begin your journey toward strength and health.

There is not just one way to approach working out. Each person has her or his own preference. I'm going to list a few different workout plans. Choose the one that feels fun for you.

Weight Training:

I am a big fan of weight training, and for women it can help to prevent illnesses like osteoporosis. Weight training requires equipment. It's not something that is easily done from home. Here is an example of what a regime might look like for weight training.

Sunday: lower body

Leg press, abductor, back kicks

Monday: upper body

Back lifts, leg lifts, pull downs, arm curls

Tuesday: lower body

Leg press, sumo squat, back kicks

Wednesday: upper body

Back lifts, crunches, free weights

Thursday: lower body

Leg press, mason twist, back kicks

Friday: upper body

Back lifts, leg lifts, pull downs, arm curls

I learned most of what I know about weight training from some pretty amazing trainers. Understanding proper form was crucial. It can be helpful to hire a trainer for one to three months to understand correct form and to learn different options for lifting. Then take what you know and use it to create the work out that is best for you.

Body Weight Resistance:

This is the perfect workout for the queen or king on a budget. It costs ZERO dollars to do this training, and I have friends that have slim, strong muscles from doing this type of workout on a daily basis. Our body is heavy! Lifting and moving it will absolutely build muscle and strength!

This training can be done six or seven days a week. The best time to do it is right when you wake up. Go to the bathroom, have a glass of water with a tablespoon of apple cider vinegar, and then begin training. This type of training only requires about five to fifteen minutes a day.

Morning Routine:

Jumps (tap your knees), jumping jacks, burpees, bicycle, mason twist, plank, push-ups, run in place or jump rope.

You can search 'body weight training' or 'hit training' online if you want more ideas. There are lots of vloggers who are fantastic at this type of training. You can follow along with their workout ideas if you enjoy that type of motivation.

This type of training is done by count rather than by repetition. So you want to set a goal to do each exercise for either thirty or sixty seconds. Afterward have some protein and repeat again tomorrow.

Cardio for Trauma:

The final way you can train is through classes. Some people love to work out with a group. An added benefit to this type of training is that it can help to calm the effects of PTSD.

People often relate PTSD to soldiers or people who have experienced a violent event. The truth is most of us have lived through a trauma. Have you ever lost a loved one, been in a car accident, experienced a breakup, broken a bone, been bullied, been in a fight at school, or experienced date rape? So many people have experienced trauma and we often don't do much to heal from those memories. But the body keeps score.

Certain exercises have helped me to reduce the symptoms of PTSD. I have noticed that if I run every evening for a half hour most of my symptoms subside. So, not only will your body become stronger with this type of exercise, but you may notice an improvement in your mood as well.

Cardio:

Running, fight training, biking, and yoga.

I throw yoga in the mix, not because it is cardio; if anything it is body weight resistance, but because it has a similar effect on the symptoms of PTSD.

Running: I recommend thirty-sixty minutes daily. Running outdoors is great because it will clear your mind and have an added spiritual affect. You might think you can't do this in the heat or snow, but I have found that it becomes almost addictive. I have come to enjoy running whether I'm sweating bullets or running through snowy hills.

Fight training: This can be boxing, mixed martial arts, or Krav Maga. I have found Krav Maga to be quite beneficial because not only do I get the cardio workout, but I also know how to defend myself even in the deadliest situations. That feels very empowering to me.

Biking: Bike riding can be done on the street or off road. Either is great. There are apps and websites that have weekly group outings that you can attend. Biking together can lead to friendships and laughter and it helps you to travel longer distances when you're with friends. I used to mountain bike with my ex boyfriend through forests and rivers. It's one of my fondest memories of our time together. It's a great way to bond with others and make friends.

Yoga: If you have never tried yoga, I highly recommend it. Yoga was one of the first workouts that helped me release my unresolved emotions. When I starting attending yoga I would sometimes cry during certain poses. For whatever reason I was able to tap in to those hidden emotions through moving and stretching my body. I find with fight training I can open my voice and express unresolved anger. With yoga I am able to express my sorrows in a safe space. You don't even have to go to a studio to do this one. There are plenty of yoga videos online that you can do at home.

Don't be strict with yourself. I tend to switch between one type of training or another depending on my budget or location. Find your groove, but remember training is not just about building strength or slimming down. It's also about maintaining a healthy mood and a happy heart!

Affirming Your Vision

―――――

By now you have signed up for a recovery group to deal with any unresolved hurts or hang-ups, you have been eating a meal plan that is helping to improve both your mental health and your physical health, and you are training daily. Wow! Look at you! You are building a strong foundation that will allow you to walk in your life's purpose with out distraction.

As I said before I believe there is a link between our physical health and our mental health. I also believe that we have to envision the life we want. If you look back at the pyramid in Session 2 you will see that after the basic needs have been met you are able to build on your friendships, family, and achievements. This method leads us down a path that results in us living out the purpose we were meant to. Trauma, loss, or heartbreak, can temporarily derail us from our purpose and goals. *From Pain to Purpose* is meant to help us return to the place of remembering what we came here to do.

Because many of us have experienced trauma in some way we have to begin to manage our self-esteem as well as our ability to hope. You can give me the best food in the world and a gym full of equipment, but if I have no hope for my future I will not meet a life partner, I will not get the job of my dreams, because I can't see it in my heart.

Let's take a moment to practice faith, hope, and trust. Holding on to a dream tightly is not the way to make it happen. It will only suffocate your dream, and people may perceive us as desperate rather than confident. The first year I did this I had a full length mirror hung on the inside of my closet door. It was surrounded by affirmations. I had literally pasted the door from top to bottom with good words about myself, and my life.

After my break up I was totally lost, not knowing which path to choose. It took me years to return to a full understanding of what my purpose was. Which tells me something about that relationship. When we are in a great partnership we empower each other's destinies. By the time I left this relationship I was so far removed from my purpose I could barely remember what it was. The word for that is co-dependency. You can learn more about that by attending a recovery meeting in your area, but I can assure you, it's never good to be in a co-dependent relationship. It will provide a false sense of security, but bear no actual fruit in your life.

Since then God has revealed to me a dream for my life. Slowly but surely, I have written thirty-six affirmations that I read out loud to myself every morning. Some of them have come true, and some of them are not yet a reality. In order to take the next step toward our purpose we have to believe it is meant for us. What is meant for us will develop when we are ready to allow it to happen.

"What then shall we say in response to this?
If God is for us, who can be against us?"
Romans 8:28-31

God wants to help you achieve your purpose in life? Your life's calling will no doubt also build up and help others. So, just let it unfold. Allow it to become your reality.

Take a moment to write out affirmations for the life you believe you are called to live. Look back at Maslow's Hierarchy of Needs and be sure to include every aspect of life in your affirmations. My list includes provisions for daily food, love and relationship, as well as career goals. And remember to include your hobbies. Hobbies can greatly increase our joy. A joyful heart is more likely to have faith and believe that good things will happen. Do not neglect having fun.

Once you have written your affirmations read them to yourself every morning. I took the time to pre-record them on my phone. When I wake up I hit play before I even set one foot on the floor. This shifts my heart in the direction that I want to focus.

Imagine what kind of a life we could lead if we understood and agreed with the vision that God has for our life? Then we would be partnering with our creator to manifest this purpose. When we are in alignment with our purpose anything is possible. Literally anything. I put outrageous things on my affirmations. I wrote, "I am the best actress in the world." "I am a billionaire and have money to help others." Is it really going to hurt anyone if I say this every day for the rest of my life? If it is meant for me, and will empower and benefit the world around me, then let it be so. Somebody has to be the queen or king. Might as well be you!

Take some time and sit down and let the spirit speak these affirmations in to your mind. Every single affirmation I wrote was something that I felt led in my heart to add. Nothing on my list is from me holding on tightly to a dream, but rather me hearing from God what my life is intended to be and agreeing with it.

For the rest of your life read these to yourself every morning, and see what unfolds.

Take A Break!

By now you have a good handle on how to care for your body, and you have been able to develop some new habits that will help you through out the rest of this process. Remember that self-care is not about perfection. I don't follow a perfect plan, perfectly, every single day. But, my intention is set to follow a good plan, most of the time.

You have worked hard these last four sessions, and opened up your heart to healing both your body and your mind. That takes courage and you should be proud of the work you have done so far.

Session 5 is all about taking a break. Believe it or not, taking a break is a big part of producing good fruit in your life. An important part of any harvest happens during a time of growing under the soil, often where no one can see it.

"Still other seed fell on good soil. It came up, grew and produced a crop, some multiplying thirty, some sixty, some a hundred times."
Mark 4:8

Sometimes making good plans means taking a break, or just breathing for a minute while God works something out on your behalf. This quiet time is crucial, and without it we will never get to where we want to be in life.

Did you ever try to watch a movie with someone who keeps talking, or asking questions? We all have that inquisitive friend who is so eager to understand things or know what's next. Honestly, I'm sometimes that friend.

This need to have all the answers is a form of resistance. Trying to get all the answers before taking a risk is about wanting to have control. It's been my experience that it is not until we relinquish our own control that we can truly begin to step in to what our lives are meant to be.

In Session 1 we let it all go; our hopes, our dreams, whatever we were holding on to so tightly. Now we are going to learn how to remember our true dreams. Our true purpose, our true desires. When we walk in agreement with what is meant for us amazing things happen. It's not about pushing to make things happen, it's about allowing good and purposeful things to become.

You may find after this session that some of the things you were holding tightly in your fist are actually correct and true dreams for your life. Sometimes it's not that we don't have the right desires in our hearts, but rather that we are doing things our own way, without inviting all the power of our creator in to the experience. You may succeed up to a point that way. You can find career advancement through working hard, you can certainly get married without knowing God, and you may even be content. But this program is not for those looking for a life of contentment. *From Pain to Purpose* is for the warriors; those who want to cross the Jordan in to the Promised Land. True queens and kings allow themselves in to positions of purpose, but are humble enough to be able to sacrificially put all that on the line to help others when the need arises.

Ultimately Esther's title did not define who she was. 'Orphan' did not define her. 'Queen' also did not define her. She was always defined by who God said she was. When our blessing comes from our source of creation, we know that we are secure because our cornerstone is true. We are not dependant on our title, or our money, or the status of our relationships. All of those things can so quickly be lost, but when we are defined by our creator, our foundation cannot be taken from us no matter what happens in this world. We'll talk more about this in chapter 6-7.

At this point in our journey I want you to go on a retreat. The specifics of that will vary for each of you. I generally take a weekend off every three months. It helps me to evaluate and hear God's voice for the next three months. Depending on my budget that looks different every time. Sometimes it's a week fishing on Lake Michigan. Sometimes it's a long drive up the coast. Sometimes it's a day trip snowboarding.

If the budget is very tight it could be sending the kids off to a relatives for a day or two, and turning your cell phone off. Take a bath, paint your nails, and eat your favorite meal. Whatever you do don't make it about finances. You'll be missing the point if you do that. It's about creating space for silence. How can we expect to hear God's voice over all the noise around us?

So take a break this month, and consider scheduling regular breaks through out the year. In this way you will build a closer relationship with God and have a great deal more clarity about the direction of your life.

I have compiled for you a worksheet to complete during this quiet time. Take your time with it. God has in mind a specific purpose for you. Allow yourself the space to hear it.

Silent Retreat Worksheet:

Quiet your mind and ask spirit to direct your thoughts before starting.

Part 1

- What is the next journey that you are called to go on?
- Is it time to begin a new journey towards something?
- • Is it time to begin to release something, or find more healing in an area of your life?

Part 2

- As you think about your journey, what steps might need to happen to begin that journey?
- Would you take some time to meditate and ask spirit to show you the next steps?

Or

- Maybe you're aware that you are already on a specific mission. Perhaps you have already begun something that you know God wants you to continue. Are there new aspects of that for you to address?

Here are some reflection questions for you to answer.

- When you think of the mistakes you have made in the past, are you tempted to run away and hide or do you feel you can turn toward your creator and community and experience love?

- What is your biggest desire today? Is there something you wish could be redeemed or something you wish you could be delivered from?

- Do you need to be strengthened in an area of your life? Are you longing for some guidance?

Focus on what is coming to the surface and then journal your thoughts.

I believe that life experience and our connection with God helps to place desires in our hearts. Sometimes we use addictions as a way of trying to fill those desires. It's ineffective and will never work. Thankfully we have recovery programs to help keep us in check when we fall in to that trap. A prayer I like to pray is "God, match the desires of my heart with the purpose for my life." To me, that is the definition of walking in peace. I want to truly desire what is best for me. I don't want to fill the gap with illusions or lesser things. Clarity is key to understanding the difference. And clarity comes from quiet time.

Time is a tricky thing. It's an illusion in it's own way. A foggy mirror we look through all the while trying to figure out what we're looking at. Don't get too attached to time. It has been my experience that things unfold in their own timing. What we perceive as lost time means nothing to the universe spinning around us. Trying to control the timing of things will diminish the power they could have had in your life if you would have let them unfold as they were meant to.

Sometimes the way we would like things to go quite frankly would not have been the best way for every one involved. For your life to be a testament to others, the kind of life people talk about hundreds of years later, you'll have to let go some of your control. Sometimes we'll never see the fruit of a ministry in our lifetime, because the harvest comes after we have passed away. Find your way to be at peace with that. We're all here as a collective group and when we do it right we can spread joy, faith, and hope in astounding ways.

Here is a quick word for the women.

"For a man is the image and glory of God...but the woman is the glory of man."
Corinthians 11:7

I know that I am valued and cherished. I know that I add beauty to this world. It is easy to feel forgotten as women, since so many writings, and stories point to assigning one gender most of the power. But I assure you, if you will sit quietly with God, you will come to understand your very own power and specific purpose and how it relates to humankind. Never let yourself be diminished by cultural norms. Both genders are purposed and powerful, unique and precious. Equally of value, but differently positioned. Remember who you are. Deep down you can feel it in those moments of silence with your creator.

This concludes Session 5. It's a very introspective and quiet session, but study it diligently. It was during this time of introspection that I found my purposes, and I reflect back to them every day. It's the difference between being in a fog and having clarity. So make this session a priority. Carve out that mini vacation. I'm excited for what God is going to reveal!

SESSION 6

Clarifying Your Purpose

You might find that after your retreat you have found some new affirmations for your life. Go back over your daily list from Session 4 and add to it as needed. It took me years to have the courage to write down the big dreams that were in my heart. It's perfectly ok to add to it or change it as your purpose becomes clearer to you.

By now you should have a pretty good idea of what you are called to do with your life. You probably always knew, but needed the time to quiet your mind and allow your heart to be open to this purpose.

If you still feel lost I recommend you read a book called *My Heart the Holy Spirit's Home* by Lynda Hunter Bjorklund. This book helped to reveal my purpose to me in a clear and distinct way that no other program has done for me. It's a bit of a slow start, but push through. It's a powerful read, and will hopefully fill in the blanks where any question marks remain.

One of two things should have revealed itself to you from last session's work. You are either already walking in your purpose, or you are waiting for some opportunities to open up. Sometimes we find ourselves walking in our destiny in some areas, and waiting in other areas. So, let's talk about what to do when we are waiting.

It was about this time during my Esther year that it all became clear to me. I began reading the book of Esther over and over. It might interest you to take some time this week to read through the story of Esther as well. This amazing story of an orphan made queen helped me to understand that I was exactly where I needed to be, and that purpose takes time.

To become the queen or king that we are intended to be we must begin to value ourselves deeply. Learning self-value cannot be rushed. I have found that many times those around me would like me to just snap out of it. That kind of pushing, or pulling toward healing was not helpful to me. It's not helpful to anyone.

My hope is that even when this time of inner preparation is complete that you still enjoy the process of finding more and more healing as you grow and expand. Whenever I feel like I'm in a hurry I take a moment to remember who God says I am. I am a cherished woman; my value is greater than the most precious stones of the earth.

Would we rush brushing the hair of the queen of England, if that was our only and most important job? Doubtful. It's more likely we would do it to the best of our ability and focus on what we were doing because all would watch and look to see if we truly valued the queen by how well we had completed the task of caring for her. Care for yourself that way! Keep adjusting your mind until you see yourself as the queen or king that you are.

In this session we are going to begin to get in to the planning and action part of these twelve months of preparation. We have built a strong foundation of body, mind, and heart and now we can take one step higher on the pyramid.

I have created a process to help you. Take out your journal. On the left of one page, right down what you believe is the purpose for your life. What are you called to do? Even if these things seem impossible write them down. I have found that God often asks me to do impossible things. Get used to it. Living a life of power often starts off as feeling impossible.

In the right hand column make a list of what you can do right now to either continue toward the goal, or to build a solid foundation during a waiting period. Let me give you an example.

In the sixth month of my Esther year I determined that I truly had a desire for marriage and motherhood. This was a little tough for me because I had divorced four years prior. I had watched several of my friends marry in the previous two years while my relationship had ended in a breakup. I had planned to have all my children by a certain age and that age had passed. So, when my prayers and meditations resulted in revealing that my greatest desire was for marriage and children I was a little unsure. If you are feeling this way, put your own ideas on the shelf for a little while. You can come back to them if you want to at a later date, but for now, let's practice trusting our own hearts. Let's look closely at the book of Esther and read back to how she followed Mordecai and Hegai's instructions.

"When the turn came for Esther to go to the king,
she asked for nothing other than what Hegai...suggested.
And Esther won the favor of everyone who saw her."
Esther 2:15

"But Esther had kept secret her family background and nationality just
as Mordecai had told her to do, for she continued to follow Mordecai's
instructions as she had done when he was bringing her up."
Esther 2:20

Nowhere does it say she questioned them or argued with them, or suggested she had a better idea. Rather it says she listened to their instructions or suggestions. If you are truly going to step in to your life's purpose, whether that's singing, writing, parenting, sales, whatever, you are going to have to trust your heart and spirit to guide you. You are going to have to let go of doubts.

I assure you no woman, man, or child has a greater mind or understanding than the spirit of our creator. The key to succeeding here is being able to hear that voice. This happens through daily moments of prayer and meditation.

Confirm what you feel and hear during these focused times, and find accountability by sharing some of your ideas with people you trust. I have found that this is the best equation to stay on a purposed path.

For me, stepping in to purpose looked like this:

- Complete a twelve-step program
- Stay sober from co-dependency
- Help other women that are already in my world
- Enjoy this time with my loved ones
- Set aside space and time that I could be alone with God

I found that for a time I needed to pull myself out of some leadership positions to get the distance I needed to heal from my breakup. I prayed daily for God to show me how to walk out the path set aside for me. I took time to evaluate what I felt, needed, and wanted in a marriage; and I prayed for protection during this time that I felt so vulnerable.

If you feel called to an area or subject where you have already previously failed, let me suggest a way to navigate that. Inventory what you did when you tried to achieve that goal on your own. Some recovery programs offer great ways to help evaluate your past choices. They will give you charts, and sponsors, and partners. These will help you to see clearly what has happened that you don't want to repeat, and what you'd like to do differently. Then you can begin anew with a fresh start.

For me, it was tricky to feel purposed to do something I had already failed at. It required trust. Trust in God and trust in people. Yes. People. Other humans are going to be part of your purpose. Our lives are not just all about us. We do what we do so that we can co-create with God and others. Esther was put in a position of power at a particular time in herstory so that she might be able to help her people. There is a higher purpose to all that we do. We are all part of a puzzle. The puzzle won't be complete unless we allow ourselves to step in to our unique purpose.

So, look for ways you can serve others, and also ways you can take better care of yourself, and add those ideas to your list.

Add these few things to your daily focus time.

1. Pray for inner guidance every day. To show you what you can do today to be headed in the right direction.

2. Whatever you feel like your purpose is, begin to pray daily for that. As I did this I began to understand

what a good husband for me might look like. What kind of person I could uniquely partner with to bring comfort to hurting people in the world. To effect change in powerful ways.

Begin to pray for others. Anyone can begin to pray for the hurting, for those who are undervalued, for orphans, or whatever it is your heart leans toward. There is no pre-qualification for prayer. You can pray for anything your heart feels connected to.

At this point you might start to feel pressure, some anxiety, or even fear. If you are feeling that way don't give it too much focus. It's hard to begin to believe in things that were once dead in your life. It takes courage, and some times we just have to do things afraid, and be willing to take a next step.

Esther invested a year of her life not knowing what the outcome would be. I imagine she might have been a little doubtful half way through. Allow yourself that. Take time to do something to pamper yourself.

You have done great work so far! You are half way through! Let's end this session celebrating how far we've come!

Praying With Intention

If you are practicing all of the suggestions given to you in the last six sessions, you may be experiencing some growing pains around this time. I'm going to list some of the things I went through in month seven of my Esther year to give you an idea of what that might look like.

- A friend of mine betrayed me, in both business and my personal life.
- I began to feel anxiety daily (which is not common for me).
- My leaders noticed my stress, and I was asked to stop participating in some things; which was probably for the best but felt like an attack at the time.

Pretty rough stuff, and all of this happened in a thirty-day timeframe. Remember that you are making some serious changes to the way you speak, the way you think, the way you operate. You are growing from an orphan in to a queen or king. Some people in your life will resist this change in you.

Even if you haven't experienced any of these types of issues, this chapter is still for you. We will be talking about growing pains, but we are also going to study how to focus our thoughts, prayers, and meditations. We will practice some specific prayers every day this month and take some time to ask spirit to heal us. Let's learn to speak life over ourselves, instead of death.

Before I begin, I want to give you some encouragement. The next two sessions will be uber focused. This is probably where you will experience the most change. There will be fun after, I promise! But, to be an effective human we have to have our minds in unity with our creator. For some of us that is going to take some practice; for others it will be more of a polishing. For me it was an intense time of adjustment!

I have one requirement before you begin the next two sessions. Surround yourself with a team. If you are already in a recovery program, use that team of people to hold you accountable for the next few weeks or even month. You want to have two-three people available to you to process with. These people should have time to return your calls, and communicate in a way that blesses you.

Some people are simply not able to easily understand me. This is usually because we do not share the same core values. We may both be dedicated to the same purpose, but communicate differently. A great way to gauge if some one is speaking your language is to ask yourself these questions. Do you feel encouraged and understood after you're done talking with this person? Do you feel like you can tell them the truth without judgment?

For example, I chose to be accountable to a woman in my community at one point in my journey. She was very popular and doing a lot for her local church. However we did not have a similar communication style. We also did not have the same internal struggles. Sharing with her left me feeling misunderstood. Try having a few casual interactions or coffee dates with someone first before inviting them to be a part of your accountability team. Be comfortable with removing people from your team if it's not working for you. It's ok to change your mind. Really, it's ok. You're never going to make any progress if you feel judged or uncomfortable.

Let's shift gears and talk about negative thinking. You might find that the dreams that you discovered in Session 5 seem impossible. You might even see things happening in your life right now that cause you to think that life is actually going in the opposite direction of this dream. These kinds of issues can open up the door for negative thinking to begin. We want to find a way to be in agreement with the purpose for our life. All of heaven and earth want you to walk in your purpose. It only benefits the world when you do so, and heaven sings. But if we don't believe that we can do it, we might suffer from anxiety, worry, or even physical illness.

The first thing we can do is speak forgiveness over those who have hurt us. Take some time to sit down, write down the things that have happened that have hurt you, and consciously make a decision to forgive the people involved. Say it out loud. Say it even if you don't mean it at all. You will mean it over time, if you stick with it, but you've got to set your intentions. Our intention before anything else is to forgive.

"Therefore, if you are offering your gift at the altar and there
remember that your brother or sister has something
against you, leave your gift there in front of the altar.
First go and be reconciled to them, then come and offer your gift."
Matthew 5:23-24

I really believe that if we want to have any forward progress as a result of our intentional prayers and meditation time, we need to forgive others for how they have hurt us. I want to forgive generously. I certainly don't want anything standing between me and my purpose.

Don't be discouraged by this process. It typically has taken me years to forgive those who wounded me deeply. I can see a difference in my heart over time. I have spoken words of forgiveness out loud hundreds of times regarding the same issue.

Sometimes I say to myself "I have already forgiven you. You can not hurt me today." My process may appear slow to those around me, but I am experiencing healing in my own way. You will too, in your own way, in your own time.

Don't worry about results. Just let it take however long it takes.

There is truth in the saying "I was not in my right mind." If you are in your 'right' mind things will come together. If you are thinking negative thoughts you may struggle to see victory in your life.

"But the fruit of the Spirit is love, joy, peace, forbearance, kindness, goodness, faithfulness, gentleness, and self-control."
Galatians 5:22-23

These are the kinds of things we want to experience in our lives. It's not about money. It's not about marriage or prestige. It's about being well deep in our souls. I'm guilty of believing that good fruit means a husband, and homes, and nice cars, and fun trips. But those all turn to ashes long after I leave this world. The people we love will return to the earth one day. A true harvest is one that happens in the heart and lasts for eternity. Things like love, joy, peace, and kindness will be remembered long after I am gone. The love I show others will remain in their hearts forever.

Add these statements to your daily meditation time and read them out loud for one month.

- I believe that good things are meant for my life.
- I will allow those good things to happen to me today.
- Let my life bring joy to the people around me.
- I am preparing my heart to be able to receive the good life and purpose that I was created for.

I want to add a thought about grieving. It is ok to grieve if we have had a loss. However we are not meant to remain in a state of grieving for our entire lives. Be intentional about asking God to lift that grief from you when the time is right.

- I have done all I can and now I surrender _____ over to you.
- If there is a desire in my heart than I know that it will come to completion.
- Please bring some one in to my day to bless me. To show me your love in a tangible way.

Many believe we should pray that last prayer for others, and we should. But right now, I want you to pray that prayer for you for thirty days, as a way to invite encouragement in to your life.

- Spirit, help me to find my significance in what you say about me.
- Bring me a peace today that passes all understanding.

That's your assignment for the next thirty days. Remember, you are not in this alone. Growing pains are temporary. There is a purpose for you right now, right where you are. Stay at your post. I guarantee you some day you will meet someone who is where you are now, and you will be able to encourage her or him because you know where they have been. Be that person to shine a light on a dark path.

Protecting Your Self Esteem

This month we are going to do some exercises to improve our self-esteem and our self-worth. No one would believe a queen was a queen if she held her head low, and spoke poorly of herself. As a king we have an opportunity to demonstrate what self-love and self-worth looks like so that others might also be empowered to value themselves. In order to be able to do that well we have to first learn how to manage and protect our own self-esteem.

There really are only two steps to having high self-esteem, speaking life over you, and protecting yourself from those who don't. Remember that...

"The tongue has the power of life and death..."
Proverbs 18:21

When I embarked on my eighth month in my Esther year I was receiving care from pastors at my local church. I had done a great deal of work in the prior seven months, and was at a point of making a serious shift in my life. At the beginning of this season I was completely and utterly bankrupt. I woke in the morning with anxiety. By the end of month six my body weight was below what I wanted it to be. I was physically and emotionally bankrupt.

I had been taking a break from a two-year relationship and my partner told me that he wanted to start dating other people. At the same time, my ex husband was emailing me several times a week criticizing me, judging me, and threatening me. A dear friend told me that I had to take a break and get some help. She described me as being just like a baby who could do no more to care for herself than to cry out for food, and sleep when she is tired. That was a pretty good description of how I felt.

With the help of some very special people in my life, I was able to get to the other side of that. Whether you are as bankrupt as I was, or whether you are experiencing sunny skies, these practices will be a benefit to you. Developing these two habits will help you to maintain a healthy level of self-esteem, and self-worth through out your lifetime. Bad things happen to everyone, but our circumstances are not a reflection of our value as a person.

The first thing that I am going to ask you to do is take another sabbatical. Who knew the path to your purpose would require you to take several holidays? I am a big believer in taking quarterly mini vacations, and at least one or two longer vacations each year. We need to quiet the voices of the world in order to be able to hear the voice of God.

If you are able to I recommend taking the whole month off of work. I left Los Angeles for nearly an entire month at this point. Some of that time I spent driving around the country seeing places I had always wanted to see. Some of it I spent at home taking hot baths and reading. I have only one requirement. Go alone.

This time is dedicated to your relationship with your creator. This is not the time for bonding with friends or lovers, or family. In order to truly understand our worth, our tightest bond must first be with the source of all that is good. Because it is from this connection that we experience joy, peace, love, and purpose. Even if you feel that you already have a strong relationship with God, you will still benefit from this time alone in the same way you benefit from family holidays or romantic getaways with your spouse. We need time alone with God to strengthen ourselves internally. The healthier we are, the better off we will be at every thing we do, and every one we love.

If you cannot take an entire month off, the bare minimum would be three days, but shoot for at least a week if you can. The more time the better.

Often we have made people and achievements our priority, but how much have we prioritized our relationship with God? If we make a person our god, they will eventually fail us, and we will become disillusioned. If we make achievements our god then our self-esteem will plummet when we don't reach our goals. Our hearts must first belong to our source. Out of that belonging grows our self-worth and our self-esteem.

During your vacation time talk to God as you would your best friend. Take pictures and leave room for God in the shot. Tell God your secrets, your dreams, your vision. Your creator is your best friend. Moving forward go to God *first* with all your needs, worries, and joys. First means before all your best friends and favorite counselors. You will instinctively know which humans to invite in to your inner world to help and guide you, but only after you have first brought your concerns to your creator.

The other thing we will be doing this session is reading this statement to ourselves every morning in the mirror out loud.

God loves me. God is proud of me. I am valuable.

It has to be out loud. Some how our brain believes what it hears us say. I imagine that is part of the way that God gave us the power of life in our tongue.

There is also another step you can take. It is a healing practice called Inner Healing Prayer. I encourage you to wait until you finish reading this book before pursuing it. This study requires a lot of focus, and it may be too much to try to work through all of that at the same time as we work through all of this.

Inner Healing Prayer is designed to get to the root of anything standing between you and your ability to connect with God. Once those blocks are removed you can walk more easily in your God given destiny. Even after you complete this book you may still have some things boiling in the subconscious that you haven't been able to locate and dig up on your own. If you sense that you need this additional healing definitely do it!

At the end of this month you will feel a deep connection to your creator. If you never had a relationship with God before reading this book it's a good idea to invite God to be a part of your life moving forward. I would recommend intentionally asking God to be a part of your process. If you feel like that's a good idea for you, here is a prayer that might help you take a step in that direction.

"I know that I cannot save myself. No longer will I close the door to my heart when I sense your spirit calling to me. By faith I gratefully receive your gifts and guidance. I am ready to trust you as my creator, guide, and source of all that is good. I am so thankful for the access that I have to you and I want to stay connected to you all of my life."

If you ever begin to feel alone again, just take a moment to remember this special time that you spent alone with God. Take time and reconnect. Don't make it harder than it has to be. Always ask God to be present in a tangible way. I believe you will sense a response to this prayer every time.

Before my month-long vacation, I had difficulty feeling a genuine connection to God. I begged God to allow me to feel close in a tangible way. The way I feel, see, and hear my friends every day. I was not disappointed. I saw many sunsets and rises, waves and winds, that seemed to be a special love note from God directly to me. Even now when I feel down I open my actual physical hand and ask God to hold it. This time alone with God shifted my journey on this earth. It's important.

There are two things that I would encourage you to do in order to maintain high self-esteem.

1. Say only good things about yourself. A great book to read on this is *I Declare* by Joel Osteen. If I catch myself cursing myself; i.e. "I don't feel well." "So and so broke up with me." "I got fired." I stop right there and rephrase. "I am going from strength to strength." "We have decided to release each other to pursue other relationships." "It looks like there might be a better option for me out there." See the difference? One is powerful, one is defeating. There is always a way to put a spin on something and make it a win for you. I never ever tell myself that I have lost, or that I am defeated. There will be losses in life, but I choose to focus on what I have, not what is missing. Because of that mindset

of abundance I always feel that I am a valuable part of this earthly kingdom.

2. Block anyone who speaks death over you. At the end of my eighth month I was feeling pretty good. I got home from traveling. I met with my counselor, and things seemed better. Then my ex husband sent me some criticizing emails. I had asked him several times over the course of years to adhere to some boundaries when communicating. To not include criticisms, name calling, or threats. It was clear he was not willing to honor the boundary I had requested. At this time, I choose to stop reading and responding to his emails all together. I even went so far as to block his number on my phone. Instead a team of friends agreed to read through any emails that I received and let me know if there was any actual action step needing to be taken. In this way, I never read his horrible words again. As the weeks and months went by I began to feel better and better about myself. It is crucial to only allow voices in your ear that bring life. Find people who encourage you and lift you up and let

them talk as much as they want. When someone criticizes you, judges you, or threatens you, make it as hard as possible for them to ever actually have any contact with you. I wish I could promise you that they will take the hint. Honestly, if they are suffering from narcissism or borderline personality disorder, they will actually fight harder to get at you. Abusive people operate under a system of power and control. If you take that away in one area they will fight, sometimes for years, to regain their perceived power over you in any way they can. But let them fight. Find prayers to protect you against your enemies and speak those prayers each night. Reading Apostle Paul's writing always comforts me.

"'My grace is sufficient in you, for my power is made perfect in weakness.'
Therefore I will boast all the more gladly about my weaknesses,
so that Christ's power may rest on me. That is why for Christ's sake,
I delight in weaknesses, in insults, in hardships, in persecutions,
in difficulties. For when I am weak, then I am strong."

This session is meant to be a powerful and life shifting time for you. Spend this time journaling and vacationing toward a deeper connection to your source. Learn how to speak life over yourself. And begin to say goodbye to people who are lowering your self-esteem. Having a foundation of self-esteem is going to launch you in to the next season of your life. With out this foundation you could find yourself back tracking. Take this session very seriously. You'll be glad you did!

Agreeing With Your Purpose

This session is going to be the first month that we truly begin to practice being a queen or king. There is not a lot of homework for this session, but it will require consistency and faith.

A few sessions back, you determined what it was that God is calling you to do with your life. For this next month you will practice agreeing with that truth that you have found in your heart. I will give you two optional ways of practicing this. You can use both if you like.

But first allow me to touch on why this practice is important. Several times in the bible God references the power of belief as well as manifestation. Jesus once met with a centurion who believed Jesus could heal his servant with out even being in the same place at the same time. Jesus noted that this centurion's belief was greater than all of Israel.

We spoke earlier about how God gave us the power of life and death in the tongue. This is a clear representation that God has given us the ability to co-create our world with God. God has given us the power to manifest and affect the world around us. It is important that we do this with intention. We are definitely going to manifest something with our words. Why not manifest a life that is in line with God's purpose for us, and also beneficial to others?

There are two ways to manifest our purpose.

Option 1:

Journal a minimum of every other day. Write out what you are thankful for in your journey that God has already provided. Be specific to the purposes that you feel have been revealed to you. For example if you are opening a store you could be thankful for the start up money, or the location, or an important contact person, or even something as simple as just getting the domain name registered. Whatever is already done, journal weekly, and start each entry by thanking God for what is already done. As new things unfold thank your creator for those new blessings. By the time I finished a year of this I had filled an entire page with blessings that were in line with the purpose for my life.

Now write out the purpose that's already in your heart. For me it was marriage. So I wrote, "I am married to a wonderful husband who is my best friend." I wrote this over and over again. You can use variations; you can use the same words, whatever works for you. If you feel your purpose is to work in human services an example might be "I am leading and mentoring women in my community to know their value."

Option 2:

Speak out loud what you are thankful for each morning. Say a thanks for what you have already been blessed with regarding your journey toward purpose. Then repeat to yourself your revealed purpose. You may repeat it many times through out the day if you like. You could put post-it notes around the house that remind you to repeat your purpose. This will help keep your vision fresh in your heart.

Repeat this process morning and night for thirty days. At the end you should feel in agreement with the specific purpose for your life. I did it almost every day for an entire year. Truth be told I still do this process morning and night for any part of my purpose that has not yet come to fruition. I will do it for years, if need be, until the promise comes. Then it goes on the 'praise report' list and I read that to myself each morning. Over the years the list of blessings really adds up. It's hard to argue with the beauty of our life when we remind ourselves of the good that has already happened.

Now you are truly walking in to your royal position as queen or king. It's ok if you experience some fear. You may have been living your life up till now as an orphan. It will take time to adjust to this new feeling of royalty.

I had a great deal of fear in my ninth month of my Esther year. It actually got worse as the month went on. The more blessing came in to my life, the more nervous I became. It was easier for me to dream about purpose than to actually see it manifesting. Especially when our purposes involve other people, which it always does. Push through this. The easiest way to release fear is to say out loud exactly how afraid you are as soon as it comes up. Then return to a place of thankfulness and agreement. You have the tools to do this.

Begin to say this mantra daily along with the other previous prayer suggestions.

"Match the desires of my heart with the purpose for my life."

This is just about the perfect prayer. When we can get ourselves to want what we were always meant for we are living a blessed life. But this will require courage. It would have been far easier for me to remain single than to learn how to be in relationship. Relationship has grown me, and matured me, in a way that I wouldn't have been able to do on my own. It allowed me to understand my preferences for my future partnership and to learn to value the things that are important to others.

Remember your team of people, and utilize those relationships this session. Use those wise voices to obtain advice, but ultimately follow the path that spirit reveals to you. God's voice is greater and truer than all the others.

Lastly, confirm your purpose through sources that are important to you. You should be able to find quotes or encouragements that are confirming the path you are on. You might find several. Post those encouragements on your walls or screen savers. It may feel like I'm asking you to write and repeat a lot. Some of you will come in to agreement with your purpose quickly. But sometimes when we experience abuse and trauma it becomes nearly impossible to believe in good things or good people. You will know how much of this to practice, because you will feel your heart shift in to agreement and peace with your purpose. Some of you will need more affirmations than others. I needed all of them!

May this session be a great blessing to you!

The Fruit Of The Spirit

A year is not really an unusual amount of time to prepare for something important. We spend four years in college studying for our careers. We often spend a year or more dating before choosing a mate. Even so, I'm sure that there may have been times when Esther felt unsure on her journey to become queen. She may have felt tired, or even lonely. There was no way for her to prove without a doubt that things would work out for her. There was no way for her to be certain that she had a great destiny ahead of her; one that would inspire us thousands of years later. Just as there is no way for us to tangibly determine if the desires in our hearts will ever happen.

So how do we live out our lives while preparing for destiny to unfold? The first thing to do is check to see if you are growing in to a person who has good character.

> "'The fruit of the spirit is love, joy, peace, forbearance, kindness, goodness, faithfulness, gentleness, and self-control."
> Galatians 5:22-23

We can have fame, we can have popularity, we can have money, career acclaim; but if we don't have character we don't have much. It is by these nine attributes that the world sees God in each of us.

There are two ways that we grow in to a person of good character. One is by letting spirit in to our heart. We do this when we make a commitment to be in constant connection to our source.

I ask every day, moment by moment, for words and inspiration as to how to live my life. Doing this over time has changed my personality in to a better, more mature woman. I love my community through encouraging words. I experience joy, often in the strangest of moments. I have peace when no one should. I forgive those who don't deserve it and show them kindness. I do good through local outreach. I have faith that positive things will happen to me. Gentleness doesn't come as easy to me, but I have my moments. And I demonstrate self-control through a healthy meal plan, and good habits.

The second way to improve your character is to walk on the path meant for you. I have found that God shines a light on my path about one step ahead. I think I would be overwhelmed if I knew the whole journey in advance. Every once in a while I get a vision of a big goal up ahead, but I never know the how or when. I do feel through prayer and meditation I know what is the next right step. If we take these next right steps each day we will find ourselves walking in our purpose month after month, year after year.

When we are walking in purpose we are closely tied to the spirit and vision meant for our life. It is as simple as following what you feel called to do. If you still aren't sure what your purpose is, try taking a personality quiz, like Meyers-Briggs or Strengths Finder. It's likely that the things we are good at and love to do are also the things we are purposed to do with our life. It's definitely a good place to start.

Now is the time to start getting excited! You are two sessions away from finishing this time of preparation! You might even find that you're a little nervous. I know my whole life I wanted to have a family of my own, but when I got two months to the end of my Esther year I started to wonder if I could be a good partner to someone. I wondered if I even had it in me. You may never be ready, but just jump anyway. And do it with your whole heart when the time comes. You'll get used to walking in purpose once you do it for a while. Then you'll wonder what you were ever doing before!

This session let's take time to do two things.

1. Let's thank God for the purpose that's in your heart. At this point I began to thank God for my future partner, and for the purposes it would fulfill to improve the world around me. I had an 'aha' moment where I realized it wasn't all about me. In that moment I dedicated my future purpose to my creator. Marriage is not my only purpose. I am also called to story telling, and advocacy for women. But during this time in my life it was important for me to focus on keeping my heart open to marriage. Even if I never married, there would be purpose in this because my experience changed me in to a person who was kinder, gentler, and filled with faith to believe in things that I couldn't prove would

ever come true. Hope is powerful and it lifts up the world around us. Hope is always a good choice.

2. Make a list of what needs to happen for you to be ready to walk straight in to what you feel your purpose is. At this point in my journey I sort of freaked out. I realized that I was not as healthy as I could be. I still had unpacked boxes in my house, even though I had moved quite some time ago. I thought for a moment, "There's no way I'm going to get all this done in two months." But, I did. I balanced my life style, and I unpacked my boxes. I didn't meet a husband at the end of the year. But I knew that I had done well to love myself better and to be open to this being a part of my purpose in life.

Do not try to become a perfect person. We will not walk in to our purpose by doing every thing perfectly. The target isn't acquired just because the bell tolls. You don't have to read in to every thing that happens as if it were a supernatural event. On December 31st my ex boyfriend (who I shared about in the introduction) invited me to spend New Year's Eve with him. I got it in to my head that

that meant he was going to be my future husband and our story of redemption would be an inspiration to all. This was not to be. Looking back I realize that he might have been a good mate for someone, but he wasn't a great mate for me. Settling is never part of our purpose.

It is only by the grace of God that I have come this far. Rely on your creator, not your own strength, and certainly not on the choices of those around you. Pray to God but definitely row to shore. God isn't in the habit of handing us every little thing our hearts desire. We have to learn to be a participant in our destiny.

Do the best that you can, and make your purpose a priority. It's important and a lot can happen in these last two sessions to build a strong foundation for your life. Focus on the end goal. See yourself there.

One more word of wisdom before we end this chapter, practice expecting the best, and thanking God for the day's blessings. Each day journal, or speak out loud, that you are going to have a great day, a great week; that you are going to be excited, that you are going to do well. At the end of each day, no matter what happened, thank God for the wonderful blessings that unfolded that day. We are going to learn to have blessing goggles during this session. If you begin to see your world as blessed it will become what you see over time.

That Pesky Devil

I'm not going to sugar coat it, this next session can be tricky. By this time some things may have shifted in your life. You are a different person than you were when you started this process. You have some idea about your life purpose, and you have the tools to get there.

We are going to do two things this session.

1. Start praying for others.
2. Address any outside attacks on our life.

Our purpose is not going to be lived out in a quiet cottage in a pasture somewhere. Unless, of course you live in a cottage with a pasture, and are called to a life of solitude. Barring that, our purpose will require us to be with other people. Start to think about the people who might be involved in helping to fulfill this purpose. Even if you haven't met all of them yet, you should have an idea what kind of person might be required to fulfill various roles.

Write out a specific prayer for each of these people, even if it's just one person, and pray for them each day. Believe for them.

"Since they could not get him to Jesus because of the crowd,
they made an opening in the roof above Jesus...
and then lowered the mat the man was lying on.
When Jesus saw their faith, he said to the paralyzed man,
'Son, your sins are forgiven.'"
Mark 2:4-5

Someone may be praying for you right now in this moment, in ways you may never know. Be that person for others. Pray over them, and speak life in to their life's purpose. This process can be especially powerful if you are praying for someone you might resent, or are angry with.

For me month eleven was a doozy! I dreamt clearly almost every night. I am gifted with an understanding of dream interpretation. My dreams helped reveal to me what ways I needed to grow. I was also dating my ex (once again), and I became angry with him as I realized he still had some addictive behaviors, and bad habits. I needed to pray for him and his part in my story. It's not fun for me to pray for someone I'm annoyed with. But it had to be done.

If you start to feel stressed, or feel self-pity, try to remember that when we walk in to the purpose and power set aside for us, some people will become uncomfortable. Some would much prefer you go back to being lost, confused, purposeless, and lacking confidence. Now that you have made some real progress toward your goals, it's possible they'll fight harder to stop you in your tracks. Ask for help if that happens. Pray for help and ask safe people that you trust. You *will* finish this intentional time of clarifying your purpose with strength and dignity.

Meditate about what more you could complete by the end of this program, and map out a plan for what you will complete over the next two sessions. Focus on what's most important. There will always be room for more growth later on. Do not pursue perfection. The illusion of perfection could cause you to give up all together. Just figure out what you can realistically do.

Some of your viewpoints may begin to change at this point. For the first time you may realize that you are better than the way you have allowed people to treat you. You are better than the way you have treated yourself. For example, I wrote in my journal "I am no longer afraid that my ex won't come back, but that I won't take him back." My understanding of my own value began to shift about this time. This is a good thing, but others might not be ready for how fast you are growing. That's ok. Just give yourself the grace that you need during this time of change.

Give yourself a victory celebration this session for how far you've come! You only have one more session of going *From Pain to Purpose*, and then you will be ready to be the queen or king of your story! Enjoy these last few moments of this powerful journey. This is a time you will look back on forever.

SESSION 12

Be Blessed!

Manage well what is already in your hands. Be faithful with what has been entrusted to you. What you are working on right now is the foundation for your purpose.

Choose to believe in people. Even if they are failing, even if they have disappointed you, choose to believe that they will come around one day. You may not be a part of their life while they're in the process, but gossip and criticism won't help them or you. When in doubt, just take the next right step. Sometimes I ask myself "Who do I want to be a year from now?" Then I make certain my choices match that future person in my mind.

You are now walking through life on purpose. Every thing that is offered to you, ask yourself; "Is this getting me closer to my dream or farther away?" "Is this on track with my purpose or will it derail me in the long run?"

I like to imagine a train riding on the tracks. It's powerful, it has a destination, and I'm on it! Is the thing I'm about to do, accept, join, tolerate, sign up for, agree with, does it fuel this purpose train, or will it derail it in the end? When I'm making tough choices I take a moment to fully imagine what it would be like for an entire train to jump of its tracks! I think about the work and delay it would take to get the whole thing back on the tracks and moving again. And once I have my answer to that question about my purpose, it's a firm yes or no. Each choice is either heading in the direction of my purpose or it's heading off the tracks. There's no in between for me.

Seek discernment in everything. It will come to you if you take the time to quiet your mind and ask for clarity. If you are praying and meditating, and you have taken your vacations, you should be able to sense direction in your life.

Ask yourself a few crucial questions.

- What do I want to change in my life?
- What has born good fruit in the last twelve months?
- What am I still trying to control and manage that doesn't belong in my hands?
- What gifts do I have that I am not using?

- What am I angry about, and am I willing to let it go?
- Do you feel like there's anything you are meant to allow in to your heart? A desire, a dream, a person? Are you going to say yes to the dream for your life?

Accept that we cannot understand everything that happens. So many times I've seen things work out that I thought would never end well. But that only happened when I stopped trying to control the situation and allowed things to unfold.

If you take anything with you from this book, let it be that you will believe in your life's purpose no matter what. This is the key to living a beautiful life. There are purposes in my heart in several different areas of life. I have no doubt that these promises will come to be. I have witnessed promises come true in my life and my friends' lives time and again.

Be sure to share your dreams with someone you trust. That way when it comes true they will have an opportunity to be inspired and filled with hope, much like I have been encouraged each time my friends married, or had a new child, or got an amazing career opportunity.

We can have a desire, a promise; something in our heart, but if we keep it a secret, no one will ever know a miracle has happened when it finally comes to fruition. Don't keep your dreams a secret. Believe in them, and allow others a chance to believe for you on the days when you grow weary or lose hope.

Several times Jesus performed miracles and asked the people to keep it a secret, but the people told anyway. Everyone gets excited when miracles happen, and when good things happen in our lives it's just impossible to keep that to ourselves.

Here are a few people in the bible who went *From Pain to Purpose*.

- Joseph went from slave to second to the king!
- Mary went from unwed mother to mother of the Son of God!
- Sarah went from childless to having a child that had many descendants!
- Ruth went from widow to married and living a blessed life!
- David went from unknown Shepherd to king!

Jessika went from a life of abuse and misuse to a life of advocating for women all around the country!

These stories are no different from yours. What is your *pain*, and what is your *purpose*? What will the story of your life be?

Expect great things. Expect expansion. Allow your world to expand in every area.

And for the love of Pete be flexible! Things have a way of happening that is beyond our imagination. Sometimes you just have to let it happen. You can try to make your blessings come true in your own way, but it won't be the best version of the blessing you could have. Just let it happen, in it's right time.

Show up for things. Show up to community events, show up to friendly gatherings, show up to school, show up to outreaches, show up for your mentees, and to your own mentor meetings. There is power in just showing up.

If your instinct is to leave something then move, quit, break up. You will know what to do. But these things should be something that you decide after meditation, prayer, and counsel.

Take your roots and dig them deep, in hope, in your community, in your family. There will be dark days, but you don't have to be alone on those days.

I still have purposes in my heart that aren't a tangible reality in my life, but that doesn't stop me from pursuing my dreams. At the end of the day, I believe my purpose is to help hurting people get from where they are to where they want to be through story telling, writing, and speaking. I am on purpose every day in every way. You reading this book right now is part of my purpose being fulfilled.

In the book of Mark a man cried out "I do believe, but help me in my unbelief!" If you're feeling doubtful seek encouragement. Scream for help if need be! Our creator holds nothing back from us. There is no lack here. You are loved so dearly, and you can give love in return.

Congratulations on your journey through these twelve sessions of preparing for your life's purpose. No matter where you're at today, or what victories and blessings you've seen, know that God is with you. You are never alone. You have come this far, and you will continue to expand as long as there is breath in you. Even if we lived a life of suffering it would be worth it to be a part of humanities great story.

My prayer for you is that you see the desires of your heart sooner than later; and that the desires of your heart always match the purpose for your life. Be blessed! Be

purposed you queens and kings! May you feel loved every
day of your journey!

Conclusion

Dearest Reader,

As I write this it has been five years since my failed relationship. In that time, my relationship with God has become so much deeper. I feel as if I am learning what a truly trusting and intimate relationship looks like.

God has shown me three purposes for my life, marriage, story telling, and advocacy. On the day that I am writing this epilogue I am not married. Three days ago I was offered the lead in a film that feels like a redemption of all that I lost in my career when I was exploited. I have been working as an advocate for the last five years with several organizations, doing outreach, writing, and speaking in order to help women who find themselves exploited by the commercial sex trade.

As you can see my life is in process. In some areas I am fully living out my purpose, in other areas it looks as if it may never happen. When I wrote the first draft of this book five years ago I had it in my head that by the end of the year I would be fully walking in my purpose in every area because I believed that in order to teach others I had to know it all. I want to tell you that that is an illusion.

I believe that if we are in agreement with God's purpose for our lives we will see those things happen in our lifetime. If God has given you a promise it will happen. I have seen it happen in my friends lives time and time again. Each time I celebrate because each time it reminds me that the promise of our dreams always comes true. And when it does, we inspire hope in those who have not yet seen their dreams redeemed.

If you take one thing away from reading this book let it be that life is a journey. Whether I am renting a room from a friend or owning my own home I am still blessed. Whether I am single year after year, or experiencing a life with a partner I am very blessed. Each moment of Esther's journey was a blessing, both to her personal growth and to others in her world. She stayed on course, she womanned her post. She took wise advice from those who cared about her. These are the things that make your life a beautiful story.

I am here to inspire, love, and help others. So are you! Let go of your timeline for when you think things should happen in your life. Just do the next right thing. Take the next right step, because all those steps have blessings in them for the queens and kings around you, and each of those steps will mature you in to the person you can be.

As I journey through my life so many people are praying for me. Community and relationships are powerful. What I do affects me, but it also affects my family and the women I mentor. Choose each step carefully. Make each choice with the people you love in mind. I could easily have gone off course in my own selfishness and impatience, but it would be better that I never marry, or work, or advocate than that I do those things from an unhealthy place.

Queen or king, you are so loved! God loves you, and the people in your world love you more than you may realize. Make it a priority to love yourself as you would your best friends. That will make your journey so much more enjoyable.

Be well sweet queen or king and know that your life is powerful and it has great meaning. You are not alone in your pain or your struggles. God is always with you.

All my love,

Jessika

Call to Action

Your journey doesn't end here. If you feel that this book has helped you and would like to help others along their journey of recovery and purpose please visit our page at **www.FromPainToPurpose.org**. There you can finds ways to connect with our community and to support the work we do.

For every book ordered a free copy will be provided to a survivor of sexual exploitation or trafficking. All proceeds from this book are dedicated to providing ways to empower and equip survivors so that they can go from surviving to thriving! Your purchase of this book has helped enable them to do that.

If you are a survivor of trafficking or exploitation please visit our site to find additional resources to help you continue on your journey toward freedom and realignment with your purpose in life. We are so glad to be on this journey with you! You are never alone!!

www.FromPainToPurpose.org

About the Author

Jessika Fuhrmaneck is a writer, public speaker and actor who has been a dedicated advocate for the support and recovery of survivors of exploitation and trafficking in the commercial sex trade.

Born and raised in Baltimore, Maryland, at the age of twenty she moved to Los Angeles to continue working in the performance arts. Throughout her childhood and her career, she experienced harassment, assault, and exploitation. She now dedicates her time and abilities to find ways to help bring restoration to others who have had similar experiences.

She is a contributing writer for online magazines and blogs, and also speaks at conferences, events, and on radio and other televised programs. Jessika's focus is helping hurting people get from where they are to where they want to be. She has partnered with several organizations including Nola Brantley Speaks, Treasures Ministry, and Saddles for Survivors.

As an author she writes books intended to empower and equip individuals, families, and communities to live their best lives. She co-authored the Christian derivative of the international Strengthening Families and Communities program and is also featured in Dr. Rachel Eva's Total Transformation workbook. Jessika is based out of Los Angeles where she works as an actress and a writer.

Printed in the USA
CPSIA information can be obtained
at www.ICGtesting.com
JSHW080001150824
68134JS00021B/2207

9 781642 799613